THE BRITISH LIBRARY

TREASURES
IN FOCUS

Shakespeare's Plays

But come let vs go, n[...] [...]
Thou hast done thy office as thou shouldst.

Exit omnes.

Enter to the Parliament.
*Enter two Heralds before, then the Duke of Buckingham, the Duke of
Suffolke, and then the Duke of Yorke, and the Cardinall of Winche-
ster, and then the King and the Queene, and then the Earle of Sa-
lisbury, and the Earle of Warwicke.*

King. I wonder our Vnkle Glofter ftayes fo long.
Queen. Can you not fee? or will you not perceiue,
How that ambitious Duke doth vfe himfelfe?
The time hath beene, but now the time is paft,
That one fo humble as Duke Humfrey was:
But now let me not meete him euen in the morne,
When euery one will giue the time of day,
Yet he will neither moue nor fpeake to ys,
See you not how the Commons follow him
In troopes, crying, God faue the good Duke Humfrey,
Honouring him as if he were their King?
Glofter is no little man in England,
And if he lift to ftirre commotions,
It is likely that the people will follow him.
My Lord, if you imagine there is no fuch thing,
Then let it paffe, and call't a Womans feare.
My Lord of Suffolke, Buckingham, and Yorke,
Difproue my allegations if you can,
And by your fpee[...]te, if you cannot proue me,
I will fubfcribe and fay, I wrong'd the Duke.
Suf. Well hath your Grace forefeene into that Duke,
And if I had beene licenc'd firft to fpeake,
I thinke I fhould haue told your Graces tale.
Smooth runnes the brooke, wheras the ftreame is deepeft.

No,

Sami[...]
That all you[...]
Is ouercome[...]
King. C[...]
but Gods [...]
Turke. C[...]
Euen as I [...]

Suf. N[...]
Vnleffe [...]
We do c[...]
*Hum[...]
Nor c[...]
Where [...]
To[...] [...]om Frãce,
And [...]
Thr[...]
So C[...]
Eu[...]
Th[...]
Be[...]
In[...]
Many a [...]
Haue I fent ouer for the [...]
Becaufe I would not racke the needie Commons.
Car. Is your Proteſtorſhip you did deuiſe
Strange torments for offenders, by which meanes
England hath beene defam'd by tyrannie.
Hum. Why tis well knowne, that whilſt I was Protector
Pitty was all the fault that was in me:
A murtherer or foule felonious Theefe,

That.

THE QUOTATIONS in this volume of *Treasures in Focus* are illustrated from the earliest printed editions of Shakespeare's plays held by the British Library. More than half are from the quartos – small, cheap pamphlets, some of which appeared in Shakespeare's lifetime. The others are from the First Folio, printed just seven years after Shakespeare's death. No manuscripts of his plays survive, so these printed editions are the closest we can come to the words Shakespeare originally wrote.

Some of the quotations have been chosen for their familiarity; others were selected for the light they throw on the play or its characters. Only the thirty-seven plays widely accepted as by Shakespeare are represented. Collaborative works, such as *The Two*

Noble Kinsmen, and those of doubtful authorship, such as *Edward III*, have been excluded, as have Shakespeare's sonnets and other poems.

Nineteen of Shakespeare's plays were printed in quarto between 1594 and 1622. When the First Folio appeared in 1623, its compilers (Shakespeare's friends and fellow-players John Heminge and Henry Condell) declared that they were publishing his plays 'according to the true original copies'. In many cases, they drew on the existing quartos, but for some plays they supplied far superior versions. Eighteen plays appeared for the first time in the First Folio. The terms 'quarto' and 'folio' refer to the way in which these books were printed. In a quarto the printed sheet is folded in half twice, to give four leaves (eight pages); in a folio it is folded once, to give two leaves (four pages).

Modern scholars have tried to identify the missing manuscripts behind the printed texts. These include authoritative sources, such as Shakespeare's foul papers (his working drafts of the plays) or the fair copies he prepared for his company, the Lord Chamberlain's Men. There were also unreliable reported texts – manuscripts prepared from memory by one or more of the actors who took part in performances.

Each quotation is illustrated from the very first printed edition of the play in the British Library. Where possible, it is reproduced at the same size as the original, and a marginal bracket indicates the lines selected. It is accompanied by the act and scene numbers and the text as these appear in *The Arden Shakespeare Complete Works* (1998). In a few cases the illustrated quotation differs from the

Arden text: for example, *King Henry VI, Part 2*, which is illustrated by the reported text of the quarto and not the First Folio text (probably from Shakespeare's foul papers) preferred by the scholarly editors of the Arden edition.

The quotations appear in an order close to that in which, so far as we know, the plays were written. Brief details of the date of creation, first performance and first publication of each play are given, taken from the most recent Arden editions of the individual plays. More information about all the plays published in quarto can be found on the British Library's website *Shakespeare in Quarto*, which is part of *Treasures in Full* (www.bl.uk).

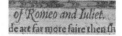

Wid. Come, come, your mocking: we will haue no telling.

Pet. Come on I say, and first begin with her.

Wid. She shall not.

Pet. I say she shall, and first begin with her.

Kate. Fie, fie, vnknit that thretaning vnkinde brow,
And dart not scornefull glances from those eies,
To wound thy Lord, thy King, thy Gouernour.
It blots thy beautie, as frosts doe bite the Meads,
Confounds thy fame, as whirlewinds shake faire budds,
And in no sence is meete or amiable.
A woman mou'd, is like a fountaine troubled,
Muddie, ill seeming, thicke, bereft of beautie,
And while it is so, none so dry or thirstie
Will daigne to sip, or touch one drop of it.
Thy husband is thy Lord, thy life, thy keeper,
Thy head, thy soueraigne : One that cares for thee,
And for thy maintenance. Commits his body
To painfull labour, both by sea and land :
To watch the night in stormes, the day in cold,
Whil'st thou ly'st warme at home, secure and safe,
And craues no other tribute at thy hands,
But loue, faire lookes, and true obedience ;

The Taming of the Shrew
Act 5, Scene 2

A woman mov'd is like a fountain troubled,
Muddy, ill-seeming, thick, bereft of beauty,
And while it is so, none so dry or thirsty
Will deign to sip or touch one drop of it.
Thy husband is thy lord, thy life, thy keeper,
Thy head, thy sovereign;

CONTEXT: The tempestuous Katherine has married
and been tamed by Petruchio. When Petruchio wins
a wager on his wife's obedience, she lectures those
assembled on wifely duty.

DATES: *The Taming of the Shrew* has been dated as
early as 1589, although 1590–1 is often suggested.
The play was originally published in the First Folio
of 1623.

King Richard III
Act 1, Scene 4

O Lord! Methought what pain it was to drown:
What dreadful noise of waters in my ears;
What sights of ugly death within my eyes!
Methoughts I saw a thousand fearful wrecks;
Ten thousand men that fishes gnaw'd upon;
Wedges of gold, great anchors, heaps of pearl,
Inestimable stones, unvalu'd jewels,
All scatter'd in the bottom of the sea.

CONTEXT: Richard, Duke of Gloucester is ambitious
to succeed his brother Edward as king. He is also
plotting to kill his other brother, the Duke of Clarence.
In this speech Clarence foresees his own death by
drowning.

DATES: *Richard III* is likely to have been written about
1591, and was perhaps first performed late that year.
The play was first published in quarto in 1597.

Vpon the hatches thence we lookt toward England,
And cited vp a thousand fearefull times,
During the wars of Yorke and Lancaster:
That had befallen vs, as we paſt along,
Vpon the giddy footing of the hatches:
Me thought that Glocester stumbled, and in stumbling
Stroke me that thought to stay him ouer board,
Into the tumbling billowes of the maine.
Lord, Lord, me thought what paine it was to drowne,
What dreadfull noise of waters in my eares,
What vgly sights of death within my eies:
Me thought I sawe a thousand fearefull wracks,
Ten thousand men, that fishes gnawed vpon,
Wedges of gold, great anchors, heapes of pearle,
Inestimable stones, vnualued Iewels,
Some lay in dead mens sculs, and in those holes,
Where eies did once inhabite, there were crept
As twere in scorne of eies reflecting gems,
Which woed the slimy bottome of the deepe,
And mockt the dead bones that lay scattered by.

Brok. Had you such leisure in the time of death,
To gaze vpon the secrets of the deepe?

Clar. Me thought I had, for still the enuious floud
Kept in my soule, and would not let it foorth,
To seeke the emptie vast and wandering aire,
But smothered it within my panting bulke,
Which almost burst to belch it in the sea.

Alarum. Excursions. Enter old
Talbot led.

Talb. Where is my other Life? mine owne is gone.
O, where's young *Talbot*? where is valiant *Iohn*?
Triumphant Death, smear'd with Captiuitie,
Young *Talbots* Valour makes me smile at thee.
When he perceiu'd me shrinke, and on my Knee,
His bloodie Sword he brandisht ouer mee,
And like a hungry Lyon did commence
Rough deeds of Rage, and sterne Impatience:
But when my angry Guardant stood alone,
Tendring my ruine, and assayl'd of none,
Dizzie-ey'd Furie, and great rage of Heart,
Suddenly made him from my side to start
Into the clustring Battaile of the French:
And in that Sea of Blood, my Boy did drench
His ouer-mounting Spirit; and there di'de
My *Icarus*, my Blossome, in his pride.

Enter with Iohn Talbot, borne.

Seru. O my deare Lord, loe where your Sonne is borne.
Tal. Thou antique Death, which laugh'st vs here to scorn,
Anon from thy insulting Tyrannie,
Coupled in bonds of perpetuitie,
Two *Talbots* winged through the lither Skie,
In thy despight shall scape Mortalitie.

O

King Henry VI, Part 1
Act 4, Scene 7

But when my angry guardant stood alone,
Tendering my ruin and assail'd of none,
Dizzy-ey'd fury and great rage of heart
Suddenly made him from my side to start
Into the clustering battle of the French;
And in that sea of blood my boy did drench
His over-mounting spirit; and there died
My Icarus, my blossom, in his pride.

CONTEXT: Henry V has been succeeded by the young
Henry VI, and England and France are at war. In this
speech the English commander, Sir John Talbot,
describes the death of his son at the siege of Bordeaux.

DATES: *Henry VI, Part 1* may have been written after
Henry VI, Part 2 and *Henry VI, Part 3*. The play was
probably first performed in 1592. It was originally
published in the First Folio of 1623.

King Henry VI, Part 2
Act 3, Scene 1

By flattery hath he won the commons' hearts,
And when he please to make commotion,
'Tis to be fear'd they all will follow him.
Now 'tis the spring, and weeds are shallow-rooted;
Suffer them now, and they'll o'ergrow the garden,
And choke the herbs for want of husbandry.
The reverent care I bear unto my lord
Made me collect these dangers in the Duke.

CONTEXT: Henry VI has recently married the French
princess Margaret against the wishes of his uncle
Humphrey, Duke of Gloucester. Here Queen Margaret
speaks of her suspicions about Gloucester's ambitions
for the throne.

DATES: *Henry VI, Part 2* was probably written by 1591
and first performed in that year. It was first published
in quarto in 1594 as *The First Part of the Contention
Betwixt the Two Famous Houses of Yorke and Lancaster*,
in a text that differs from the better-known version
printed in the First Folio in 1623.

Enter to the Parliament.

ter two Heralds before, then the Duke of Buckingham, the Duke of Suffolke, and then the Duke of Yorke, and the Cardinall of Winche-ster, and then the King and the Queene, and then the Earle of Sa-lisbury, and the Earle of Warwicke.

King. I wonder our Vnkle Gloster stayes so long.

Queene. Can you not see? or will you not perceiue,
ow that ambitious Duke doth vse himselfe?
e time hath beene, but now the time is past,
at none so humble as Duke Humfrey was:
t now let one meete him euen in the morne,
hen euery one will giue the time of day,
t he will neither moue nor speake to vs.
e you not how the Commons follow him
troopes, crying, God saue the good Duke Humfrey,
onouring him as if he were their King?
loster is no little man in England,
nd if he list to stirre commotions,
is likely that the people will follow him.
y Lord, if you imagine there is no such thing,
hen let it passe, and call't a Womans feare.
y Lord of Suffolke, Buckingham, and Yorke,
isproue my allegations if you can,
nd by your speeches, if you can reproue me,
will subscribe and say, I wrong'd the Duke.

Suf. Well hath your Grace foreseene into that Duke,
nd if I had beene licenc'd first to speake,
thinke I should haue told your Graces tale.

And if the rest be true that I haue heard,
Thou cam'st into the world   *He stabs him.*

   Glo. Die Prophet in thy speach, Ile heare no more,
For this, amongst the rest, was I ordainde.

   Hen. I and for much more slaughter after this.
O God forgiue my sinnes, and pardon thee.   *He dies.*

   Glo. What? will the aspyring blood of *Lancaster*
Sinke into the ground? I had thought it would haue mounte
See how my sword weepes for the poore Kings death,
Now may such purple teares be alwayes shed,
For such as seeke the downefall of our house.
If any sparke of life remaine in thee,

                   Stabbe him againe.

Downe, downe to hell, and say I sent thee thither.
I that haue neither pittie, loue, nor feare:
Indeed twas true that *Henrie* tolde me of,
For I haue often heard my mother say,
That I came into the worlde with my legges forward:
And had I not reason thinke you to make haste,
And seeke their ruines that vsurpt our rights?
The women wept, and the Mid-wife cride,
O Iesus blesse vs, he is borne with teeth.
And so I was indeed: which plainely signifie,
That I should snarle and bite, and play the dogge.
Then since Heauen hath made my body so,
Let Hell make crookt my minde, to answere it.
I had no father; I am like no father.
I haue no brother; I am like no brothers.

King Henry VI, Part 3
Act 5, Scene 6

The midwife wonder'd, and the women cried
'O Jesu bless us, he is born with teeth!'
And so I was, which plainly signified
That I should snarl, and bite, and play the dog.
Then, since the heavens have shap'd my body so,
Let hell make crook'd my mind to answer it.

CONTEXT: Henry VI and Edward IV have been fighting
for the throne as civil war rages in England. Edward's
brother Richard, Duke of Gloucester, has just murdered
King Henry. Here he reveals his villainy in a soliloquy.

DATES: *Henry VI, Part 3* must have been written by
1592, and was probably first performed before June
that year. The play was first published in octavo in
1595 as *The True Tragedie of Richard Duke of York, and
the Death of Good King Henrie the Sixt,* in a text that
differs from the better-known version printed in the
First Folio in 1623.

Titus Andronicus
Act 5, Scene 2

Here stands the spring whom you have stained
    with mud,
This goodly summer with your winter mixed.
You killed her husband, and for that vile fault
Two of her brothers were condemned to death,
My hand cut off and made a merry jest,
Both her sweet hands, her tongue, and that
    more dear
Than hands or tongue, her spotless chastity,
Inhuman traitors, you constrained and forced.

CONTEXT: Lavinia, daughter of the Roman general
Titus Andronicus, has been raped and mutilated by the
sons of the Roman empress Tamora. Titus now has
them at his mercy, and bitterly recites their crimes
before cutting their throats.

16

DATES: *Titus Andronicus* was probably written in late
1593. The play's first recorded performance was very
early in 1594, and it was published in quarto the
same year.

Enter Titus Andronicus with a knife, and Lauinia
with a Bason.

Titus. Come, come *Lauinia*, looke, thy foes are bound,
Sirs stop their mouthes, let them not speake to me,
But let them heare what fearefull words I vtter.
Oh villaines, *Chiron* and *Demetrius*,
Here stands the spring whome you haue staind with mud,
This goodly Sommer with your Winter mixt,
You kild her husband, and for that vilde fault,
Two of her brothers were condemnd to death,
My hand cut off, and made a merry iest,
Both her sweet hands, her tongue, and that more deere
Then hands or tongue, her spotlesse chastity,
Inhumaine traytors, you constraind and forst.
What would you say if I should let you speake?
Villaines for shame you could not beg for grace.
Harke wretches how I meane to martyr you,
This one hand yet is left to cut your throates
Whilst that *Lauinia* tweene her stumps doth hold
The Bason that receaues your guilty blood.
You know your Mother meanes to feast with me,
And calls herselfe Reuenge, and thinkes me mad.
Harke villaines, I will grinde your bones to dust,
And with your blood and it Ile make a paste

For fo he will'd it.

Baft. Thither fhall it then,
And happily may your fweet felfe put on
The lineall ftate, and glorie of the Land,
To whom with all fubmiffion on my knee,
I do bequeath my faithfull feruices
And true fubiection euerlaftingly.

Sal. And the like tender of our loue wee make
To reft without a fpot for euermore.

Hen. I haue a kinde foule, that would giue thankes,
And knowes not how to do it, but with teares.

Baft. Oh let vs pay the time : but needfull woe,
Since it hath beene before hand with our greefes.
This England neuer did, nor neuer fhall
Lye at the proud foote of a Conqueror,
But when it firft did helpe to wound it felfe.
Now, thefe her Princes are come home againe,
Come the three corners of the world in Armes,
And we fhall fhocke them : Naught fhall make vs rue,
If England to it felfe, do reft but true.   *Exeunt.*

King John
Act 5, Scene 7

Come the three corners of the world in arms
And we shall shock them! Nought shall make us rue
If England to itself do rest but true!

CONTEXT: A threatened French invasion of England
has failed, and King John has just died. In the final
speech of the play, the Bastard Faulconbridge declares
that England will never be conquered if only the
country stands firm against its enemies.

DATES: *King John* has been dated as early as 1590–1,
although it is usually thought to date between 1593
and 1596. The play was originally published in the
First Folio of 1623.

The Two Gentlemen of Verona
Act 2, Scene 4

I have done penance for contemning Love,
Whose high imperious thoughts have punish'd me
With bitter fasts, with penitential groans,
With nightly tears, and daily heart-sore sighs,
For in revenge of my contempt of Love,
Love hath chas'd sleep from my enthralled eyes,
And made them watchers of mine own heart's sorrow.

CONTEXT: Valentine, a young gentleman of Verona
who has hitherto dismissed the power of love, has
fallen in love with Silvia. In this speech he describes
his suffering on her account.

DATES: *The Two Gentlemen of Verona* was probably
written before 1598, and perhaps dates to the early
1590s. It was originally published in the First Folio
of 1623.

Sil. And dutie neuer yet did want his meed.
Seruant, you are welcome to a worthlesse Mistresse.

Pro. Ile die on him that saies so but your selfe.

Sil. That you are welcome?

Pro. That you are worthlesse.   (you.

Thur. Madam, my Lord your father wold speak with

Sil. I wait vpon his pleasure : Come Sir *Thurio*,
Goe with me : once more, new Seruant welcome ;
Ile leaue you to confer of home affaires,
When you haue done, we looke too heare from you.

Pro. Wee'll both attend vpon your Ladiship.

Val. Now tell me : how do al from whence you came?

Pro. Your frends are wel, & haue thē much cōmended.

Val. And how doe yours ?

Pro. I left them all in health.

Val. How does your Lady ? & how thriues your loue ?

Pro. My tales of Loue were wont to weary you,
I know you ioy not in a Loue-discourse.

Val. I *Protheus*, but that life is alter'd now,
I haue done pennance for contemning Loue,
Whose high emperious thoughts haue punish'd me
With bitter fasts, with penitentiall grones,
With nightly teares, and daily hart-sore sighes,
For in reuenge of my contempt of loue,
Loue hath chas'd sleepe from my enthralled eyes,
And made them watchers of mine owne hearts sorrow.
O gentle *Protheus*, Loue's a mighty Lord,

Ant. What wilt thou flout me thus vnto my face
Being forbid? There take you that sir knaue.

E.Dro. What meane you sir, for God sake hold your
Nay, and you will not sir, Ile take my heeles. (hands:

Exeunt Dromio Ep.

Ant. Vpon my life by some deuise or other,
The villaine is ore-wrought of all my monie.
They say this towne is full of cosenage:
As nimble Iuglers that deceiue the eie:
Darke working Sorcerers that change the minde:
Soule-killing Witches, that deforme the bodie:
Disguised Cheaters, prating Mountebankes;
And manie such like liberties of sinne:
If it proue so, I will be gone the sooner:
Ile to the Centaur to goe seeke this slaue,
I greatly feare my monie is not safe.   *Exit.*

Actus Secundus.

Enter Adriana, wife to Antipholis Sereptus, with
Luciana her Sister.

Adr. Neither my husband nor the slaue return'd,
That in such haste I sent to seeke his Master?

The Comedy of Errors
Act 1, Scene 2

The villain is o'er-raught of all my money.
They say this town is full of cozenage,
As nimble jugglers that deceive the eye,
Dark-working sorcerers that change the mind,
Soul-killing witches that deform the body,
Disguised cheaters, prating mountebanks,
And many such-like liberties of sin:

CONTEXT: Twin brothers both named Antipholus, and
their twin servants both called Dromio, have grown up
separately in Ephesus and Syracuse. When they all
come together in Ephesus there is much confusion
because of mistaken identities. Here Antipholus of
Syracuse suspects his own servant of stealing his
money, unaware that he has been speaking to Dromio
of Ephesus.

DATES: The first recorded performance of *The Comedy
of Errors* was in 1594. Its creation has been variously
dated between 1589 and 1594. The play was originally
published in the First Folio of 1623.

Love's Labour's Lost
Act 4, Scene 3

Consider what you first did swear unto,
To fast, to study, and to see no woman;
Flat treason 'gainst the kingly state of youth.
Say, can you fast? your stomachs are too young,
And abstinence engenders maladies.

CONTEXT: The King of Navarre and his companions
have sworn to devote themselves to study and to avoid
women for three years. When the Princess of France
and her ladies arrive on a visit, the young men are
unable to keep their vows. Here the witty Berowne
makes excuses for their conduct.

DATES: *Love's Labour's Lost* is usually dated to 1594–5.
It was first published in quarto in 1598.

Consider what you first did sweare vnto:
To fast, to study, and to see no woman:
Flat treason gainst the kingly state of youth,
Say, Can you fast? your stomacks are too young:
And abstinence ingenders maladies.
And where that you haue vowd to studie (Lordes)
In that each of you haue forsworne his Booke.
Can you still dreame and poare and thereon looke.
For when would you my Lord, or you, or you,
Haue found the ground of Studies excellence,
Without the beautie of a womans face?
From womens eyes this doctrine I deriue,
They are the Ground, the Bookes, the Achadems,
From whence doth spring the true *Promethean* fire.
Why vniuersall plodding poysons vp
The nimble spirites in the arteries,
As motion and long during action tyres
The sinnowy vigour of the trauayler.
Now for not looking on a womans face,
You haue in that forsworne the vse of eyes:
And studie too, the causer of your vow.
For where is any Authour in the worlde,
Teaches such beautie as a womas eye:
Learning is but an adiunct to our selfe,
And where we are, our Learning likewise is.
Then when our selues we see in Ladies eyes,

Be not her maide since she is enuious,
Her vestall liuery is but sicke and greene,
And none but fooles do weare it, cast it off:
It is my Lady, ô it is my loue, ô that she knew she wer,
She speakes, yet she saies nothing, what of that?
Her eye discourses, I will answere it:
I am too bold, tis not to me she speakes:
Two of the fairest starres in all the heauen,
Hauing some busines to entreate her eyes,
To twinckle in their spheres till they returne.
What if her eyes were there, they in her head,
The brightnesse of her cheek wold shame those stars,
As day-light doth a lampe, her eye in heauen,
Would through the ayrie region streame so bright,
That birds would sing, and thinke it were not night:
See how she leanes her cheeke vpon her hand.
O that I were a gloue vpon that hand,
That I might touch that cheeke.

 Iu. Ay me.
 Ro. She speakes.
Oh speake againe bright Angel, for thou are
As glorious to this night being ore my head,
As is a winged messenger of heauen
Vnto the white vpturned wondring eyes,
Of mortalls that fall backe to gaze on him,
When he bestrides the lazie puffing Cloudes,
And sayles vpon the bosome of the ayre.

 Iuli. O *Romeo, Romeo,* wherefore art thou *Romeo?*
Denie thy father and refuse thy name:

Romeo and Juliet
Act 2, Scene 2

Two of the fairest stars in all the heaven,
Having some business, do entreat her eyes
To twinkle in their spheres till they return.
What if her eyes were there, they in her head?
The brightness of her cheek would shame those stars
As daylight doth a lamp. Her eyes in heaven
Would through the airy region stream so bright
That birds would sing and think it were not night.
See how she leans her cheek upon her hand.
O that I were a glove upon that hand,
That I might touch that cheek.

CONTEXT: Romeo and Juliet have fallen in love,
although their families are bitter enemies. Here Romeo
is enraptured by the sight of Juliet as she stands on the
balcony outside her room.

DATES: *Romeo and Juliet* can be plausibly dated to
1595. The play was first published in quarto in 1597.

King Richard II
Act 2, Scene 1

This happy breed of men, this little world,
This precious stone set in the silver sea,
Which serves it in the office of a wall,
Or as a moat defensive to a house,
Against the envy of less happier lands;
This blessed plot, this earth, this realm, this England,

CONTEXT: John of Gaunt disapproves of his nephew
King Richard's government. Sick and dying, he speaks
lovingly of the realm of England.

DATES: *Richard II* was probably written about 1595.
The play was first published in quarto in 1597.

Then all too late comes Counſell to be heard,
Where will doth mutiny with wits regard:
Direct not him whoſe way himſelfe wil chuſe,
Tis breath thou lackſt, and that breath wilt thou looſe.

    Gaunt Me thinkes I am a prophet new inſpirde,
And thus expiring do foretell of him,
His raſh fierce blaze of ryot cannot laſt:
For violent fires ſoone burne out themſelues,
Small ſhoures laſt long, but ſodaine ſtormes are ſhort:
He tires betimes that ſpurs too faſt betimes
With eagre feeding foode doth choke the feeder,
Light vanitie inſatiate cormorant,
Conſuming meanes ſoone praies vpon it ſelfe:
This royall throne of Kings, this ſceptred Ile,
This earth of maieſtie, this ſeate of Mars,
This other Eden, demy Paradice,
This fortreſſe built by Nature for her ſelfe,
Againſt infection and the hand of warre,
This happy breede of men, this little world,
This precious ſtone ſet in the ſiluer ſea,
Which ſerues it in the office of a wall,
Or as moate defenſiue to a houſe,
Againſt the enuie of leſſe happier lands.
This bleſſed plot, this earth, this realme, this England,
This nurſe, this teeming wombe of royall Kings,
Feard by their breed, and famous by theyr byrth,
Renowned for theyr deedes as far from home,
For chriſtian ſeruice, and true chiualry,

Quin. Let vs heare, sweete *Bottom.*

Bot. Not a word of mee, All that I will tell you, is
the Duke hath dined. Get your apparrell together,
strings to your beardes, new ribands to your pu
meete presently at the palace, euery man looke ore hi
For, the short and the long is, our play is preferd, l
case let *Thisby* haue cleane linnen: and let not him
plaies the Lyon, pare his nailes: for they shall har
for the Lyons clawes. And most deare Actors, eate n
nions, nor garlicke: for we are to vtter sweete breath
I do not doubt but to heare them say, it is a sweete Cor
No more wordes. Away, go away.

Enter Theseus, Hyppolita, *and* Philostrate.

Hip. Tis strange, my *Theseus*, that these louers spea
The. More straunge then true. I neuer may beleeue
These antique fables, nor these Fairy toyes.
Louers, and mad men haue such seething braines,
Such shaping phantasies, that apprehend more,
Then coole reason euer comprehends. The lunatick
The louer, and the Poet are of imagination all comp
One sees more diuels, then vast hell can holde:
That is the mad man. The louer, all as frantick,
Sees *Helens* beauty in a brow of *Ægypt.*
The Poets eye, in a fine frenzy, rolling, doth glance
From heauen to earth, from earth to heauen. And as
Imagination bodies forth the formes of things

A Midsummer Night's Dream
Act 5, Scene 1

Lovers and madmen have such seething brains,
Such shaping fantasies, that apprehend
More than cool reason ever comprehends.
The lunatic, the lover, and the poet
Are of imagination all compact:

CONTEXT: Theseus has just heard about the strange
adventures of two young couples of his court during
a night in the woods around Athens. He muses on the
madness of lovers.

DATES: *A Midsummer Night's Dream* was probably
written in 1595 or 1596. The play was first published
in quarto in 1600.

King Henry IV, Part 1
Act 2, Scene 4

Thou art violently carried away from grace, there is a devil haunts thee in the likeness of an old fat man, a tun of man is thy companion. Why dost thou converse with that trunk of humours, that bolting-hutch of beastliness, that swollen parcel of dropsies, that huge bombard of sack, that stuffed cloak-bag of guts, that roasted Manningtree ox with the pudding in his belly, that reverend vice, that grey iniquity, that father ruffian, that vanity in years?

CONTEXT: King Henry disapproves of his son's riotous behaviour with the dissolute Sir John Falstaff. During a drinking spree, Prince Henry pretends to be his father and in this speech admonishes Falstaff for his gluttony.

DATES: *King Henry IV, Part 1* was probably written in late 1596 or early 1597, shortly before its first performance. It was first published in quarto in 1598 as *The History of Henrie the Fourth*. In the First Folio of 1623, the play was retitled *The First Part of Henry the Fourth*.

Prin. Doſt thou ſpeake like a king, do thou ſtand for me, and ile play my father.

Fal. Depoſe me, if thou doſt it halfe ſo grauely, ſo maieſtically, both in word and matter, hang me vp by the heeles for a rabbet ſucker, or a poulters Hare

Prin. Well, here I am ſet.

Fal. And here I ſtand, iudge my maiſters.

Prin. Now Harry, whence come you?

Fal. My noble Lord from Eaſtcheape.

Prin. The complaints I heare of thee are greeuous.

Fal. Zbloud my Lord they are falſe: nay ile tickle ye for a yong prince I faith.

Prin. Sweareſt thou vngratious boy, hence forth nere looke on me, thou art violently carried awaie from grace, there is a diuell haunts thee in the likeneſſe of an olde fat man, a tun of man is thy companion: why doeſt thou conuerſe with that trunke of humours, that boultinghutch of beaſtlineſſe, that ſwolne parcell of dropſies that huge bombard of ſacke, that ſtuft cloakebag of guts, that roſted Manningtre Oxe with the pudding in his belly, that reuerent vice, that gray iniquity, that father ruffian, that vanity in yeares, wherein is he good, but to taſt ſacke and drinke it? wherein neat and clenly, but to carue a capon and eat it? wherein cunning, but in craft? wherein crafty, but in villany? wherein villanous, but in al things? where in worthy, but in nothing?

Fal. I would your grace would take me with you, whome meanes your grace?

Prin. That villanous abhominable miſleader of youth, Falſtaffe that olde white bearded Sathan

War. Lesse noyse, lesse noyse.   *Enter Harry*

Prince Who saw the duke of Clarence?

Clar. I am here brother, ful of heauinesse.

Prince How now, raine within doores, and none abro
How doth the King?

Hum. Exceeding ill.

Prince Heard he the good newes yet? tell it him.

Hum. He vttred much vpon the hearing it,

Prince If he be sicke with ioy, heele recouer without p
sicke.

War. Not so much noyse my Lords, sweete prince, spe
lowe, the King your father is disposde to sleepe.

Cla. Let vs withdraw into the other roome.

War. Wilt please your Grace to go along with vs?

Prince No, I wil sit and watch heere by the King.
Why doth the Crowne lie there vpon his pillow,
Being so troublesome a bedfellow?
O polisht perturbation! golden care!
That keepst the ports of Slumber open wide
To many a watchfull night, sleepe with it now!
Yet not so sound, and halfe so deeply sweete,
As he whose brow (with homely biggen bound)
Snores out the watch of night. O maiestie!
When thou dost pinch thy bearer, thou dost sit
Like a rich armour worne in heate of day,
That scaldst with safty (by his gates of breath)

King Henry IV, Part 2
Act 4, Scene 5

Why doth the crown lie there upon his pillow,
Being so troublesome a bedfellow?
O polish'd perturbation! golden care!
That keep'st the ports of slumber open wide
To many a watchful night! Sleep with it now:
Yet not so sound, and half so deeply sweet,
As he whose brow with homely biggen bound
Snores out the watch of night.

CONTEXT: King Henry and his son are estranged, and
the king lies dying. As he sleeps, Prince Henry comes
to his bedside and, seeing the crown beside him,
meditates on the heavy burdens of a king.

DATES: *Henry IV, Part 2* can plausibly be dated to 1597
and was certainly completed before the end of 1598.
The play was first published in quarto in 1600 as *The
Second Part of Henrie the Fourth*.

The Merchant of Venice
Act 5, Scene 1

How sweet the moonlight sleeps upon this bank!
Here will we sit, and let the sounds of music
Creep in our ears – soft stillness and the night
Become the touches of sweet harmony:
Sit Jessica, – look how the floor of heaven
Is thick inlaid with patens of bright gold,

CONTEXT: Shylock has lost his case for a pound
of Antonio's flesh, the penalty he demanded of the
merchant for defaulting on his loan. He has also
lost his daughter to Lorenzo. Here Lorenzo lovingly
persuades Jessica to sit and enjoy the beauty of
the night.

DATES: The creation of *The Merchant of Venice* can be
dated between 1596 and 1598. The play had certainly
been performed by 1598. It was first published in
quarto in 1600.

Loren. Let's in, and there expect their comming.
And yet no matter : why should we goe in.
My friend *stephen*, signifie / pray you
vvithin the house, your mistres is at hand,
and bring your musique foorth into the ayre.
How sweet the moone-light sleepes vpon this banke,
heere will we sit, and let the sounds of musique
creepe in our eares soft stilnes, and the night
become the tutches of sweet harmonie :
sit *Iessica*, looke how the floore of heauen
is thick inlayed with pattens of bright gold,
there's not the smallest orbe which thou beholdst
but in his motion like an Angell sings,
still quiting to the young eyde Cherubins ;
such harmonie is in immortall soules,
but whilst this muddy vesture of decay
dooth grosly close it in, we cannot heare it :
Come hoe, and wake *Diana* with a himne,
vvith sweetest tutches pearce your mistres eare,
and draw her home with musique.   *play Musique.*

Iess. I am neuer merry when I heare sweet musique.
Loren. The reason is, your spirits are attentiue :
for doe but note a wild and wanton heard
or race of youthfull and vnhandled colts
fetching mad bounds, bellowing and neghing loude,
vvhich is the hote condition of their blood,
if they but heare perchance a trumpet sound,
or any ayre of musique touch their eares,

no addition to her wit, nor no great argument of her follie, f
I will be horribly in loue with her, I may chaunce haue for
odde quirkes and remnants of witte broken on me, because
haue railed so long against marriage : but doth not the app
tite alter? a man loues the meate in his youth, that he cannot
dure in his age . Shall quippes and sentences, and these pap
bullets of the brain awe a man from the carreere of his humo
No, the world must be peopled . When I saide I woulde di
batcheller, I did not think I should liue til I were married, he
comes Beatrice: by this day, shees a faire lady, I doe spie for
markes of loue in her.

Enter Beatrice.

Beatr. Aganst my will I am sent to bid you come in to d
ner.

Bene. Faire Beatrice, I thanke you for your paines.

Beat. I tooke no more paines for those thankes, then y
take paines to thanke me, if it had bin painful I would not ha
come.

Bene. You take pleasure then in the message.

Beat. Yea iust so much as you may take vppon a kni
point, and choake a daw withall: you haue no stomach signi
fare you well.   *exit.*

Bene. Ha, against my will I am sent to bid you come in
dinner: theres a double meaning in that: I took no more pain
for those thanks thē you took pains to thank me, thats as mu
as to say, any pains that I take for you is as easy as thanks: if I
not take pitty of her I am a villaine, if I do not loue her I am
Iew, I will go get he picture.   *exit.*

Much Ado About Nothing
Act 2, Scene 3

I may chance have some
odd quirks and remnants of wit broken on me because
I have railed so long against marriage: but doth not
the appetite alter? A man loves the meat in his youth
that he cannot endure in his age.

CONTEXT: Beatrice and Benedick are sworn enemies
to love and to each other. Benedick's friends play a trick
on him, allowing him to eavesdrop as they discuss how
much Beatrice loves him. Hearing this, Benedick begins
to fall in love with her.

DATES: *Much Ado About Nothing* was probably written in
1598–9. The play was first published in quarto in 1600.

King Henry V
Act 4, Scene 3

We few, we happy few, we band of brothers.
For he today that sheds his blood with me
Shall be my brother; be he ne'er so vile,
This day shall gentle his condition.
And gentlemen in England now abed
Shall think themselves accursed they were not here,
And hold their manhoods cheap whiles any speaks
That fought with us upon Saint Crispin's day.

CONTEXT: England is at war with France, and the
English army is on campaign. Before the Battle of
Agincourt, King Henry fires the valour of his soldiers
with this rousing speech.

DATES: *Henry V* was probably written and performed in
1599. The play was first published in quarto in 1600.

Then shall we in their flowing bowles
Be newly remembred. *Harry* the King,
Bedford and *Exeter*, *Clarence* and *Gloster*,
Warwick and *Yorke*,
Familiar in their mouthes as houshold words.
This story shall the good man tell his sonne;
And from this day, vnto the generall doome:
But we in it shall be remembred.
We fewe, we happie fewe, we bond of brothers,
For he to day that sheads his blood by mine,
Shalbe my brother: be he nere so base,
This day shall gentle his condition.
Then shall he strip his sleeues, and shew his skars,
And say, these wounds I had on Crispines day:
And Gentlemen in England now a bed,
Shall thinke themselues accurst,
And hold their manhood cheape,
While any speake that fought with vs
Vpon Saint Crispines day.

 Glost. My gracious Lord,
The French is in the field.

 Kin. Why all things are ready, if our minds be so.

 War. Perish the man whose mind is backward now.

 King. Thou dost not wish more help frō England cousen?

 War. Gods will my Liege, would you and I alone,
Without more helpe, might fight this battle out.

Bru. Thy Master is a Wife and Valiant Romane,
I neuer thought him worfe :
Tell him, fo pleafe him come vnto this place
He fhall be fatisfied : and by my Honor
Depart vntouch'd.

Ser. Ile fetch him prefently.   *Exit Seruant.*

Bru. I know that we fhall haue him well to Friend.

Caffi. I wifh we may : But yet haue I a minde
That feares him much : and my mifgiuing ftill
Falles fhrewdly to the purpofe.

Enter Antony.

Bru. But heere comes *Antony* :
Welcome *Mark Antony.*

Ant. O mighty *Cæfar* ! Doft thou lye fo lowe ?
Are all thy Conquefts, Glories, Triumphes, Spoiles,
Shrunke to this little Meafure ? Fare thee well.
I know not Gentlemen what you intend,
Who elfe muft be let blood, who elfe is ranke :
If I my felfe, there is no houre fo fit
As *Cæfars* deaths houre ; nor no Inftrument
Of halfe that worth, as thofe your Swords ; made rich
With the moft Noble blood of all this World.
I do befeech yee, if you beare me hard,
Now, whil'ft your purpled hands do reeke and fmoake,
Fulfill your pleafure. Liue a thousand yeeres,
I fhall not finde my felfe fo apt to dye.
No place will pleafe me fo, no meane of death,
As heere by *Cæfar*, and by you cut off,

Julius Caesar
Act 3, Scene 1

O mighty Caesar! dost thou lie so low?
Are all thy conquests, glories, triumphs, spoils,
Shrunk to this little measure? Fare thee well.
I know not, gentlemen, what you intend,
Who else must be let blood, who else is rank:
If I myself, there is no hour so fit
As Caesar's death's hour; nor no instrument
Of half that worth as those your swords, made rich
With the most noble blood of all this world.

CONTEXT: Julius Caesar has been assassinated by
Brutus and his fellow conspirators. Mark Antony
sorrowfully addresses Caesar's corpse and begs the
conspirators to kill him too.

DATES: *Julius Caesar* was probably written to open the
new Globe Theatre in London in 1599. The play was
originally published in the First Folio of 1623.

As You Like It
Act 4, Scene 1

Say a day, without the ever. No, no, Orlando,
men are April when they woo, December when they
wed. Maids are May when they are maids, but the sky
changes when they are wives.

CONTEXT: Orlando and Rosalind have fallen in love,
but she has been forced to flee from court to the Forest
of Arden disguised as a boy. She and Orlando meet in
the forest. He does not recognise her, and agrees to woo
her as if she were Rosalind. Here Rosalind warns him of
the transience of love.

DATES: *As You Like It* was probably written and first
performed in 1599. The play was originally published
in the First Folio of 1623.

Rof. I, but when?

Orl. Why now, as faſt as ſhe can marrie vs.

Rof. Then you muſt ſay, I take thee *Roſalind* for wife.

Orl. I take thee *Roſalind* for wife.

Rof. I might aske you for your Commiſſion, But I doe take thee *Orlando* for my husband : there's a girle goes before the Prieſt, and certainely a Womans thought runs before her actions.

Orl. So do all thoughts, they are wing'd.

Rof. Now tell me how long you would haue her, after you haue poſſeſt her?

Orl. For euer, and a day.

Rof. Say a day, without the euer: no, no *Orlando*, men are Aprill when they woe, December when they wed : Maides are May when they are maides, but the sky chan-ges when they are wiues : I will bee more iealous of thee, then a Barbary cocke-pidgeon ouer his hen, more clamorous then a Parrat againſt raine, more new-fang-led then an ape, more giddy in my deſires, then a mon-key : I will weepe for nothing, like *Diana* in the Foun-taine, & I wil do that when you are diſpos'd to be merry: I will laugh like a Hyen, and that when thou art inclin'd to ſleepe.

Orl. But will my *Roſalind* doe ſo?

catch.

Which of you knowes *Foord* of this Towne?

Pist. I ken the wight, he is of substance good.

Fal. Well my honest Lads, Ile tell you what
I am about.

Pist. Two yards and more.

Fal. No gibes now *Pistoll*: indeed I am two yards
In the wast, but now I am about no wast:
Briefly, I am about thrift you rogues you,
I do intend to make loue to *Foords* wife,
I espie entertainment in her. She carues, she
Discourses. She giues the lyre of inuitation,
And euery part to be construed rightly is, I am
Syr *Iohn Falstaffes*.

Pist. He hath studied her well, out of honestie
Into English.

Fal. Now the report goes, she hath all the rule
Of her husbands purse. She hath legians of angels.

Pist. As many diuels attend her.
And to her boy say I.

Fal. Heere's a Letter to her. Heeres another to
misteris *Page*.

Who

The Merry Wives of Windsor
Act 1, Scene 3

No quips now, Pistol. Indeed, I am in the
waist two yards about, but I am now about no waste: I
am about thrift. Briefly, I do mean to make love to
Ford's wife. I spy entertainment in her: she discourses,
she carves, she gives the leer of invitation; I can
construe the action of her familiar style, and the
hardest voice of her behaviour, to be Englished
rightly, is, 'I am Sir John Falstaff's'.

CONTEXT: Sir John Falstaff is indulging himself with
riotous behaviour in Windsor. He needs money, and
decides he can repair his fortunes (and satisfy his
lechery) by seducing the respectable Mistress Ford.

DATES: *The Merry Wives of Windsor* is unlikely to have
been written before late 1599 or 1600. The comedy
was first published in quarto in 1602.

Hamlet
Act 1, Scene 3

This above all: to thine own self be true,
And it must follow as the night the day
Thou canst not then be false to any man.

CONTEXT: Polonius is councillor of state to the new
King Claudius of Denmark, who is stepfather and
uncle to Prince Hamlet. Here Polonius lectures his son
Laertes on appropriate conduct while the young man
is in France.

DATES: *Hamlet* has been dated to 1600, although it was
apparently revised by the addition of topical references
in 1601. The play was first published in a 'bad' quarto
edition in 1603. The 'good' quarto of 1604/5 (illustrated
opposite) has a text that is nearly twice as long and
often quite different.

Of each new hatcht vnfledgd courage,
Of entrance to a quarrell, but being in,
Bear't that th'opposed may beware of thee,
Giue euery man thy eare, but fewe thy voyce,
Take each mans censure, but reserue thy iudgement,
Costly thy habite as thy purse can by,
But not exprest in fancy; rich not gaudy,
For the apparrell oft proclaimes the man
And they in Fraunce of the best ranck and station,
Or of a most select and generous, chiefe in that:
Neither a borrower nor a lender boy,
For loue oft looses both it selfe, and friend,
And borrowing dulleth edge of husbandry;
This aboue all, to thine owne selfe be true
And it must followe as the night the day
Thou canst not then be false to any man:
Farwell, my blessing season this in thee.
 Laer. Most humbly doe I take my leaue my Lord.
 Pol. The time inuests you goe, your seruants tend.
 Laer. Farwell *Ophelia*, and remember well
What I haue sayd to you.
 Ophe. Tis in my memory lockt
And you your selfe shall keepe the key of it.
 Laer. Farwell.   *Exit Laertes.*
 Pol. What ist *Ophelia* he hath sayd to you?
 Ophe. So please you, something touching the Lord *Hamlet.*
 Pol. Marry well bethought
Tis tolde me he hath very oft of late
Giuen priuate time to you, and you your selfe
Haue of your audience beene most free and bountious.

O stay and heare, your true loues coming,
That can sing both high and low.
Trip no further prettie sweeting.
Iourneys end in louers meeting,
Euery wise mans sonne doth know.

An. Excellent good, ifaith.

To. Good, good.

Clo. What is loue, tis not heereafter,
Present mirth, hath present laughter:
What's to come, is still vnsure.
In delay there lies no plentie,
Then come kisse me sweet and twentie:
Youths a stuffe will not endure.

An. A mellifluous voyce, as I am true knight.

To. A contagious breath.

An. Very sweet, and contagious ifaith.

To. To heare by the nose, it is dulcet in contagion. But shall we make the Welkin dance indeed? Shall wee rowze the night-Owle in a Catch, that will drawe three soules out of one Weauer? Shall we do that?

And. And you loue me, let's doo't: I am dogge at a Catch.

Clo. Byrlady sir, and some dogs will catch well.

An. Most certaine: Let our Catch be, *Thou Knaue.*

Clo. Hold thy peace, thou Knaue knight. I shall be con-strain'd in't, to call thee knaue, Knight.

An. 'Tis not the first time I haue constrained one to call me knaue. Begin foole: it begins, *Hold thy peace.*

Twelfth Night
Act 2, Scene 3

What is love? 'Tis not hereafter,
Present mirth has present laughter:
What's to come is still unsure.
In delay there lies no plenty,
Then come kiss me, sweet and twenty:
Youth's a stuff will not endure.

CONTEXT: While Viola (disguised as a boy) woos
Olivia on behalf of Duke Orsino, Olivia's kinsman
Sir Toby Belch and his companions make merry
elsewhere. The clown Feste entertains them with
a song about love and the passing of youth.

DATES: *Twelfth Night* was probably written and
performed in 1601. The play was originally published
in the First Folio of 1623.

Troilus and Cressida
Act 1, Scene 3

Take but degree away, untune that string,
And hark what discord follows. Each thing melts
In mere oppugnancy; the bounded waters
Should lift their bosoms higher than the shores,
And make a sop of all this solid globe;

CONTEXT: The Greeks have been besieging Troy for
seven years. They are weary of fighting, and beginning
to quarrel among themselves. One of their generals,
Ulysses, is renowned for his cleverness. He warns them
that unless they maintain their hierarchy of command
they will be beaten by the Trojans.

DATES: *Troilus and Cressida* was probably written in late
1601. The play was first published in quarto in 1609.

But by degree stand in authentique place :
Take but degree away, vntune that string,
And harke what discord followes, each thing melts
In meere oppugnancie: the bounded waters
Should lift their bosomes higher then the shores,
And make a sop of all this solid globe:
Strength should be Lord of imbecilitie,
And the rude sonne should strike his father dead.
Force should be right or rather right and wrong,
(*Betweene whose endlesse iarre Iustice recides*)
Should loose their names, and so should Iustice to ?
Then euery thing include it selfe in power,
Power into will, will into appetite,
And appetite an vniuersall Woolfe,
(So doubly seconded with will and power,)
Must make perforce an vniuersall prey,
And last eate vp himselfe.
    Great *Agamemnon*,
This *chaos* when degree is suffocate,
Followes the choaking.
And this neglection of degree it is,
That by a pace goes backward with a purpose
It hath to clime. The generalls disdaind,
By him one step below, he by the next,
That next by him beneath, so euery step,
Exampl'd by the first pace that is sick
Of his superior, growes to an enuious feauer

Emillia, runne you to the Cittadell,
And tell my Lord and Lady what has hapt:
Will you goe on, I pray, this is the night,
That either markes me, or foredoes me quite.

Exeunt.

Enter Othello *with a light.*

Oth. It is the cause, it is the cause, my soule,
Let me not name it to you, you chaste starres:
It is the cause, yet I'le not shed her blood,
Nor scarre that whiter skin of hers, then snow,
And smooth, as monumentall Alablaster;
Yet she must die, else shee'll betray more men,
Put out the light, and then put out the light:
If I quench thee, thou flaming minister,
I can againe, thy former light restore,
Should I repent me; but once put out thine,
Thou cunning patterne of excelling nature,
I know not where is that promethian heate,
That can thy light returne: when I haue pluckt the rose,
I cannot giue it vitall growth againe,
It must needes wither; I'le smell it on the tree,
A balmy breath, that doth almost perswade
Iustice her selfe to breake her sword once more,
Be thus, when thou art dead, and I will kill thee,
And loue thee after: once more, and this the last.   *He*
So sweete was ne're so fatall: I must weepe,   *kisses her.*
But they are cruell teares; this sorrowes heauenly,
It strikes when it does loue: she wakes.

Des. Who's there? Othello?

Othello
Act 5, Scene 2

It is the cause, it is the cause, my soul!
Let me not name it to you, you chaste stars,
It is the cause. Yet I'll not shed her blood
Nor scar that whiter skin of hers than snow
And smooth as monumental alabaster:

CONTEXT: The Moor Othello, a general in the service
of Venice, has married the Venetian noblewoman
Desdemona. His ensign Iago has stirred up Othello's
jealousy by insinuating that Desdemona is unfaithful.
Here Othello struggles with his desire to kill
Desdemona.

DATES: *Othello* has been dated between mid-1601 and
mid-1602. The play was first printed in quarto in 1622.

All's Well That Ends Well
Act 4, Scene 2

When midnight comes, knock at my chamber window;
I'll order take my mother shall not hear.
Now will I charge you in the band of truth,
When you have conquer'd my yet maiden bed,
Remain there but an hour, nor speak to me.
My reasons are most strong and you shall know them
When back again this ring shall be deliver'd;

CONTEXT: Helena has cured the King of France of a
deadly illness, and at the king's command won Bertram
in marriage. Bertram has refused to accept her as his
wife unless she gains his ring and conceives a child by
him. Diana, loved by Bertram, agrees to sleep with him,
knowing that Helena will take her place.

DATES: The creation of *All's Well That Ends Well* has been
plausibly dated to 1603–4. The play was originally
published in the First Folio of 1623.

Bequeathed downe from many Ancestors,
Which were the greatest obloquie i'th world,
In mee to loose. Thus your owne proper wisedome
Brings in the Champion honor on my part,
Against your vaine assault.

    Ber. Heere, take my Ring,
My house, mine honor, yea my life be thine,
And Ile be bid by thee.

    Dia. When midnight comes, knocke at my cham-
      ber window :
Ile order take, my mother shall not heare.
Now will I charge you in the band of truth,
When you haue conquer'd my yet maiden-bed,
Remaine there but an houre, nor speake to mee:
My reasons are most strong, and you shall know them,
When backe againe this Ring shall be deliuer'd :
And on your finger in the night, Ile put
Another Ring, that what in time proceeds,
May token to the future, our past deeds.
Adieu till then, then faile not : you haue wonne
A wife of me, though there my hope be done.

    Ber. A heauen on earth I haue won by wooing thee.

    Di. For which, liue long to thank both heauen & me,
You may so in the end.
My mother told me iust how he would

And doe him right, that answering one foule wrong
Liues not to act another. Be satisfied;
Your Brother dies to morrow; be content.

   Isab. So you must be ȳ first that giues this sentence,
And hee, that suffers: Oh, it is excellent
To haue a Giants strength: but it is tyrannous
To vse it like a Giant.

   Luc. That's well said.

   Isab. Could great men thunder
As *Ioue* himselfe do's, *Ioue* would neuer be quiet,
For euery pelting petty Officer
Would vse his heauen for thunder;
Nothing but thunder: Mercifull heauen,
Thou rather with thy sharpe and sulpherous bolt
Splits the vn-wedgable and gnarled Oke,
Then the soft Mertill: But man, proud man,
Drest in a little briefe authoritie,
Most ignorant of what he's most assur'd,
(His glassie Essence) like an angry Ape
Plaies such phantastique tricks before high heauen,
As makes the Angels weepe: who with our spleenes,
Would all themselues laugh mortall.

   Luc. Oh, to him, to him wench: he will relent,
Hee's comming: I perceiue't.

   Pro. Pray heauen she win him.

Measure for Measure
Act 2, Scene 2

> But man, proud man,
> Dress'd in a little brief authority,
> Most ignorant of what he's most assur'd –
> His glassy essence – like an angry ape
> Plays such fantastic tricks before high heaven
> As makes the angels weep;

CONTEXT: During the absence of Duke Vincentio, Angelo rules Vienna and has decided to enforce the law against prostitution. He has condemned Claudio to death for getting a young woman with child. Here Claudio's sister Isabella begs Angelo for mercy.

DATES: *Measure for Measure* was probably written and first performed in 1604. The play was originally published in the First Folio of 1623.

King Lear
Act 3, Scene 4

Poor naked wretches, wheresoe'er you are,
That bide the pelting of this pitiless storm,
How shall your houseless heads and unfed sides,
Your looped and windowed raggedness, defend you
From seasons such as these? O, I have ta'en
Too little care of this.

CONTEXT: King Lear has divided his kingdom between
his two eldest daughters, thinking to enjoy a carefree
retirement. When both daughters try to restrict his
remaining power, he is enraged and seeks freedom in
the open countryside in the midst of a raging storm.
As he goes mad, Lear understands the sufferings of his
poorest subjects.

DATES: *King Lear* was probably written in 1605 or 1606.
The earliest known performance was in late 1606. The
play was first published in quarto in 1608.

Is it not as this mouth ſhould teare this hand
For lifting food to't? but I will puniſh ſure,
No I will weepe no more, in ſuch a night as this!
O *Regan, Gonorill,* your old kind father   (lies
Whoſe franke heart gaue you all: O that way madnes
Let me ſhun that, no more of that.

   Kent. Good my Lord enter.

   Lear. Prethe goe in thy ſelfe, ſeeke thy one eaſe;
This tempeſt will not giue me leaue to ponder
On things would hurt me more, but ile goe in:
Poore naked wretches, where ſo ere you are
That bide the pelting of this pittiles night,
How ſhall your houſe-leſſe heads, and vnfed ſides,
Your loopt, and windowed raggednes defend you
From ſeaſons ſuch as theſe? O I haue tane
Too little care of this, take phyſicke pompe,
Expoſe thy ſelfe to feele what wretches feele,
That thou mayſt ſhake the ſuperflux to them,
And ſhew the heauens more iuſt.

   Foole. Come not in here Nunckle, her's a ſpirit, helpe me, helpe
mee.

   Kent. Giue me thy hand, whoſe there?

   Foole. A ſpirit, he ſayes, his nam's poore *Tom.*

   Kent. What art thou that doſt grumble there in the ſtraw,
come forth?

   Edg. Away, the fowle fiend followes me, thorough the ſharpe
hathorne blowes the cold wind, goe to thy cold bed and warme
thee.

And one cry'd Murther, that they did wake each other:
I stood, and heard them: But they did say their Prayers,
And addrest them againe to sleepe.

Lady. There are two lodg'd together.

Macb. One cry'd God blesse vs, and Amen the other,
As they had seene me with these Hangmans hands:
Listning their feare, I could not say Amen,
When they did say God blesse vs.

Lady. Consider it not so deepely.

Mac. But wherefore could not I pronounce Amen?
I had most need of Blessing, and Amen stuck in my throat.

Lady. These deeds must not be thought
After these wayes: so, it will make vs mad.

Macb. Me thought I heard a voyce cry, Sleep no more:
Macbeth does murther Sleepe, the innocent Sleepe,
Sleepe that knits vp the rauel'd Sleeue of Care,
The death of each dayes Life, sore Labors Bath,
Balme of hurt Mindes, great Natures second Course,
Chiefe nourisher in Life's Feast.

Lady. What doe you meane?

Macb. Still it cry'd, Sleepe no more to all the House:
Glamis hath murther'd Sleepe, and therefore *Cawdor*
Shall sleepe no more: *Macbeth* shall sleepe no more.

Lady. Who was it, that thus cry'd? why worthy *Thane*,
You doe vnbend your Noble strength, to thinke
So braine-sickly of things: Goe get some Water,

And

Macbeth
Act 2, Scene 2

Methought, I heard a voice cry, 'Sleep no more!
Macbeth does murther Sleep,' – the innocent Sleep;
Sleep, that knits up the ravell'd sleave of care,
The death of each day's life, sore labour's bath,
Balm of hurt minds, great Nature's second course,
Chief nourisher in life's feast; –

CONTEXT: Macbeth has been promised the Scottish
throne by a trio of witches. He has just murdered King
Duncan. Here he confesses his torments of fear and
guilt to his accomplice, Lady Macbeth.

DATES: *Macbeth* has been dated to 1606. The play was
originally published in the First Folio of 1623.

Antony and Cleopatra
Act 2, Scene 2

Age cannot wither her, nor custom stale
Her infinite variety. Other women cloy
The appetites they feed, but she makes hungry
Where most she satisfies; for vilest things
Become themselves in her, that the holy priests
Bless her when she is riggish.

CONTEXT: The Roman commander Mark Antony, lover
of Cleopatra the Queen of Egypt, has returned to his
wife Octavia and renewed his alliance with her brother
Octavius Caesar. Antony's follower Enobarbus
describes Cleopatra's powerful sexual allure to two of
Caesar's men.

DATES: *Antony and Cleopatra* was probably completed
by Christmas 1606–7. The play was originally
published in the First Folio of 1623.

Eno. I saw her once

Hop forty Paces through the publicke streete,
And hauing lost her breath, she spoke, and panted,
That she did make defect, perfection,
And breathlesse powre breath forth.

   Mece. Now *Anthony*, must leaue her vtterly.

   Eno. Neuer he will not :
Age cannot wither her, nor custome stale
Her infinite variety : other women cloy
The appetites they feede, but she makes hungry,
Where most she satisfies. For vildest things
Become themselues in her, that the holy Priests
Blesse her, when she is Riggish.

   Mece. If Beauty, Wisedome, Modesty, can settle
The heart of *Anthony* : *Octauia* is
A blessed Lottery to him.

   Agrip. Let vs go. Good *Enobarbus*, make your selfe
my guest, whilst you abide heere.

   Eno. Humbly Sir I thanke you.   *Exeunt*

    Enter Anthony, Cæsar, Octauia betweene them.

   Anth. The world, and my great office, will
Sometimes deuide me from your bosome.

   Octa. All which time, before the Gods my knee shall
bowe my prayers to them for you.

   Anth. Goodnight Sir. My *Octauia*
Read not my blemishes in the worlds report :
I haue not kept my square, but that to come
Shall all be done byth'Rule : good night deere Lady.

The Oakes beare Mast, the Briars Scarlet Heps,
The bounteous Huswife Nature, on each bush,
Layes her full Messe before you. Want? why Want?

    _1_ We cannot liue on Grasse, on Berries, Water,
As Beasts, and Birds, and Fishes.

    _Ti._ Nor on the Beasts themselues, the Birds & Fishes,
You must eate men. Yet thankes I must you con,
That you are Theeues profest: that you worke not
In holier shapes: For there is boundlesse Theft
In limited Professions. Rascall Theeues
Heere's Gold. Go, sucke the subtle blood o'th'Grape,
Till the high Feauor seeth your blood to froth,
And so scape hanging. Trust not the Physitian,
His Antidotes are poyson, and he slayes
Moe then you Rob: Take wealth, and liues together,
Do Villaine do, since you protest to doo't.
Like Workemen, Ile example you with Theeuery:
The Sunnes a Theefe, and with his great attraction
Robbes the vaste Sea. The Moones an arrant Theefe,
And her pale fire, she snatches from the Sunne.
The Seas a Theefe, whose liquid Surge, resolues
The Moone into Salt teares. The Earth's a Theefe,
That feeds and breeds by a composture stolne
From gen'rall excrement: each thing's a Theefe.
The Lawes, your curbe and whip, in their rough power

Timon of Athens
Act 4, Scene 3

The sun's a thief, and with his great attraction
Robs the vast sea; the moon's an arrant thief,
And her pale fire she snatches from the sun;
The sea's a thief, whose liquid surge resolves
The moon into salt tears; the earth's a thief,
That feeds and breeds by a composture stol'n
From gen'ral excrement; each thing's a thief.

CONTEXT: The rich and powerful Timon of Athens
has been ruined by his thoughtless generosity.
Deserted by his former friends, he has come to hate
mankind. When he recovers his fortune by finding
a cache of gold, bandits try to steal it. In this bitter
speech, Timon urges them to theft and murder.

DATES: *Timon of Athens* has been dated to 1607–8.
The play was originally published in the First Folio
of 1623.

Pericles

Act 5, Scene 1

Lest this great sea of joys rushing upon me
O'erbear the shores of my mortality,
And drown me with their sweetness. O, come hither,
Thou that beget'st him that did thee beget;
Thou that wast born at sea, buried at Tharsus,
And found at sea again.

CONTEXT: Pericles, Prince of Tyre, has been told that
his daughter Marina is dead. In fact, she has survived
attempted murder and capture by pirates. When she is
summoned to help Pericles, who is ill with grief, she
does not recognise him. When he learns her identity,
he is overcome with joy.

DATES: *Pericles* is believed to have been written by
Shakespeare in collaboration with another (uncertain)
author, probably in late 1607 or early 1608. The play
was first printed in quarto in 1608, but was omitted
from the First Folio of 1623.

Hell. Hoe, *Hellicanus?*

Hel. Calls my Lord.

Per. Thou art a graue and noble Counseller,
Most wise in generall, tell me if thou canst, what this mayde
is, or what is like to bee, that thus hath made mee
weepe.

Hel. I know not, but heres the Regent sir of *Metaline*,
speakes nobly of her.

Lys. She neuer would tell her parentage,
Being demaunded, that she would sit still and weepe.

Per. Oh *Hellicanus*, strike me honored sir, giue mee a
gash, put me to present paine, least this great sea of ioyes ru-
shing vpon me, ore-beare the shores of my mortalitie, and
drowne me with their sweetnesse: Oh come hither,
thou that begetst him that did thee beget,
Thou that wast borne at sea, buried at *Tharsus*,
And found at sea agen, O *Hellicanus*,
Downe on thy knees, thanke the holie Gods as loud
As thunder threatens vs, this is *Marina.*
What was thy mothers name? tell me, but that
for truth can neuer be confirm'd inough,
Though doubts did euer sleepe.

Mar. Frist sir, I pray what is your title?

Per. I am *Pericles* of *Tyre*, but tell mee now my
Drownd Queenes name, as in the rest you sayd,
Thou hast beene God-like perfit, the heir of kingdomes,

More holy, and profound, then mine owne life,
My deere Wiues estimate, her wombes encrease,
And treasure of my Loynes: then if I would
Speake that.

    Sicin. We know your drift. Speake what?

    Bru. There's no more to be said, but he is banish'd
As Enemy to the people, and his Countrey.
It shall bee so.

    All. It shall be so, it shall be so.

    Corio. You common cry of Curs, whose breath I hate,
As reeke a'th'rotten Fennes: whose Loues I prize,
As the dead Carkasses of vnburied men,
That do corrupt my Ayre : I banish you,
And heere remaine with your vncertaintie.
Let euery feeble Rumor shake your hearts :
Your Enemies, with nodding of their Plumes
Fan you into dispaire : Haue the power still
To banish your Defenders, till at length
Your ignorance (which findes not till it feeles,
Making but reseruation of your selues,
Still your owne Foes) deliuer you
As most abated Captiues, to some Nation
That wonne you without blowes, despising
For you the City. Thus I turne my backe;
There is a world elsewhere.

        Exeunt Coriolanus, Cominius, with Cumalijs.
      They all shout, and throw vp their Caps.

Coriolanus
Act 3, Scene 3

You common cry of curs! whose breath I hate
As reek o'th' rotten fens, whose loves I prize
As the dead carcasses of unburied men
That do corrupt my air: I banish you!
And here remain with your uncertainty!

CONTEXT: The victorious Roman general Caius
Martius Coriolanus has been chosen as consul by the
patricians. He has unwillingly humbled himself to gain
the citizens' vote, but when he is challenged he reveals
his contempt for the plebeians with this deliberately
insulting speech.

DATES: *Coriolanus* is usually dated between 1605 and
1610, and may have been performed in 1608. The play
was originally published in the First Folio of 1623.

Cymbeline
Act 2, Scene 2

> On her left breast
> a mole cinque-spotted: like the crimson drops
> I'th' bottom of a cowslip. Here's a voucher,
> Stronger than ever law could make; this secret
> Will force him think I have pick'd the lock, and ta'en
> The treasure of her honour.

CONTEXT: Posthumus, recently married to Cymbeline's daughter Imogen, has wagered with Iachimo on her chastity. Iachimo has been smuggled into Imogen's bedroom in a chest. Here he gazes on her and commits to memory the signs with which he will persuade Posthumus that she has been unfaithful.

DATES: *Cymbeline* has been dated between 1606 and 1611, with 1608 or 1609 as the most likely dates for its composition. The play was originally published in the First Folio of 1623.

Aboue ten thousand meaner Moueables
Would testifie, t'enrich mine Inuentorie.
O sleepe, thou Ape of death, lye dull vpon her,
And be her Sense but as a Monument,
Thus in a Chappell lying. Come off, come off;
As slippery as the Gordian-knot was hard.
'Tis mine, and this will witnesse outwardly,
As strongly as the Conscience do's within:
To'th' madding of her Lord. On her left brest
A mole Cinque-spotted: Like the Crimson drops
I'th' bottome of a Cowslippe. Heere's a Voucher,
Stronger then euer Law could make; this Secret
Will force him thinke I haue pick'd the lock, and t'ane
The treasure of her Honour. No more: to what end?
Why should I write this downe, that's riueted,
Screw'd to my memorie. She hath bin reading late,
The Tale of *Tereus*, heere the leaffe's turn'd downe
Where *Philomele* gaue vp. I haue enough,
To'th' Truncke againe, and shut the spring of it.
Swift, swift, you Dragons of the night, that dawning
May beare the Rauens eye: I lodge in feare,
Though this a heauenly Angell: hell is heere.

Clocke strikes.
Exit.

One, two, three: time, time.

Scena Tertia.

Of the beast *Calliban*, and his confederates
Against my life: the minute of their plot
Is almost come: Well done, auoid: no more.

Fer. This is strange: your fathers in some passion
That workes him strongly.

Mir. Neuer till this day
Saw I him touch'd with anger, so distemper'd.

Pro. You doe looke (my son) in a mou'd sort,
As if you were dismaid: be cheerefull Sir,
Our Reuels now are ended: These our actors,
(As I foretold you) were all Spirits, and
Are melted into Ayre, into thin Ayre,
And like the baselesse fabricke of this vision
The Clowd-capt Towres, the gorgeous Pallaces,
The solemne Temples, the great Globe it selfe,
Yea, all which it inherit, shall dissolue,
And like this insubstantiall Pageant faded
Leaue not a racke behinde: we are such stuffe
As dreames are made on; and our little life
Is rounded with a sleepe: Sir, I am vext,
Beare with my weakenesse, my old braine is troubled:
Be not disturb'd with my infirmitie,
If you be pleas'd, retire into my Cell,
And there repose, a turne or two, Ile walke
To still my beating minde.

Fer. Mir. We wish your peace.   *Exit.*

The Tempest
Act 4, Scene 1

Our revels now are ended. These our actors,
As I foretold you, were all spirits, and
Are melted into air, into thin air:
And, like the baseless fabric of this vision,
The cloud-capp'd towers, the gorgeous palaces,
The solemn temples, the great globe itself,
Yea, all which it inherit, shall dissolve,
And, like this insubstantial pageant faded,
Leave not a rack behind.

CONTEXT: Prospero, Duke of Milan, overthrown by
his brother Antonio, is in exile on a deserted island
with his daughter Miranda. By magic, he captures
his enemies, including his brother and his nephew
Ferdinand. Here Prospero ends the entertainment
that he has conjured for Ferdinand and Miranda.

DATES: *The Tempest* was probably written between late
1610 and its first recorded performance in late 1611.
The play was originally published in the First Folio
of 1623.

The Winter's Tale
Act 2, Scene 1

>   There may be in the cup
> A spider steep'd, and one may drink, depart,
> And yet partake no venom (for his knowledge
> Is not infected); but if one present
> Th'abhorr'd ingredient to his eye, make known
> How he hath drunk, he cracks his gorge, his sides,
> With violent hefts. I have drunk, and seen the spider.

CONTEXT: Leontes, King of Sicily, mistakenly believes that his wife Hermione has been unfaithful to him with Polixenes, King of Bohemia. In this speech he reveals his irrational jealousy and hysterical fear of cuckoldry.

DATES: *The Winter's Tale* was probably written and first performed early in 1611. The play was originally published in the First Folio of 1623.

Mam. There was a man.

Her. Nay, come sit downe : then on.

Mam. Dwelt by a Church-yard : I will tell it softly,
Yond Crickets shall not heare it.

Her. Come on then, and giu't me in mine eare.

Leon. Was hee met there ? his Traine ? *Camillo* with
him ?

Lord. Behind the tuft of Pines I met them, neuer
Saw I men scowre so on their way : I eyed them
Euen to their Ships.

Leo. How blest am I
In my iust Censure ? in my true Opinion ?
Alack, for lesser knowledge, how accurs'd,
In being so blest ? There may be in the Cup
A Spider steep'd, and one may drinke ; depart,
And yet partake no venome : (for his knowledge
Is not infected) but if one present
Th'abhor'd Ingredient to his eye, make knowne
How he hath drunke, he cracks his gorge, his sides
With violent Hefts : I haue drunke, and seene the Spider.
Camillo was his helpe in this, his Pandar :
There is a Plot against my Life, my Crowne ;
All's true that is mistrusted : that false Villaine,
Whom I employ'd, was pre-employ'd by him :
He ha's discouer'd my Designe, and I
Remaine a pinch'd Thing ; yea, a very Trick

His Greatnesse is a ripening, nippes his roote,
And then he fals as I do. I haue ventur'd
Like little wanton Boyes that swim on bladders:
This many Summers in a Sea of Glory,
But farre beyond my depth: my high-blowne Pride
At length broke vnder me, and now ha's left me
Weary, and old with Seruice, to the mercy
Of a rude streame, that must for euer hide me.
Vaine pompe, and glory of this World, I hate ye,
I feele my heart new open'd. Oh how wretched
Is that poore man, that hangs on Princes fauours?
There is betwixt that smile we would aspire too,
That sweet Aspect of Princes, and their ruine,
More pangs, and feares then warres, or women haue;
And when he falles, he falles like Lucifer,
Neuer to hope againe.

Enter Cromwell, standing amazed.

Why how now *Cromwell?*

Crom. I haue no power to speake Sir.

Car. What, amaz'd
At my misfortunes? Can thy Spirit wonder
A great man should decline. Nay, and you weep
I am falne indeed.

Crom. How does your Grace?

Card. Why well: